Hot Chocolate Recipes

Hot Chocolate Recipes That'll Make You Swear Off Dry Mix Forever

Copyright © 2020

DEDICATION

Contents

Liquid Gold Tahini Hot Chocolate

YIELD: 4 SERVINGS

INGREDIENTS

1 1/2 cups whole milk

1/2 cup tahini

2–3 tablespoons honey, to taste

1/2 teaspoon vanilla extract

1/2 teaspoon espresso powder

1/8 teaspoon cinnamon

1/8 teaspoon salt

8 ounces bittersweet chocolate, roughly chopped

whipped cream, for topping

sesame seeds, for topping

INSTRUCTIONS

In a small saucepan over low heat, whisk together the milk, tahini, honey (starting with 2 tablespoons), vanilla extract, espresso powder, cinnamon, and salt. Heat until the milk is just shy of scalding, then remove from heat and add in chopped chocolate.

Allow to sit for 5 minutes before whisking together. At that point, the chocolate should be fully melted, but if it isn't, place back on heat for 1 minute. If you like your hot chocolate sweeter, taste and add another tablespoon honey.

Pour tahini hot chocolate into small mugs. Top with whipped cream and sesame seeds and serve!

Kahlúa Hot Chocolate

yield: 2 SERVINGS

prep time: 5 MINUTES

cook time: 5 MINUTES

total time: 10 MINUTES

INGREDIENTS:

2 cups milk

2 tablespoons sugar

1 1/2 tablespoons Dutch-processed unsweetened cocoa powder

1/4 teaspoon cinnamon

Pinch of nutmeg

1 ounce Kahlúa coffee liqueur

Mini marshmallows, for serving

Salted caramel, for serving

Chocolate syrup, for serving

INSTRUCTIONS

In a medium saucepan, combine milk, sugar, cocoa powder, cinnamon and nutmeg over medium heat until heated through, about 2-3 minutes. Remove from heat and stir in Kahlúa.

Serve immediately, garnished with mini marshmallows, salted caramel and chocolate syrup, if desired.

French Hot Chocolate

Prep time: 2 mins

Cook time: 10 mins

Total time: 12 mins

Serves: 4

INGREDIENTS

2 cups whole milk

½ cup heavy cream

1 tablespoon powdered sugar

12 oz dark chocolate

Whipped cream

INSTRUCTIONS

Add milk, powdered sugar and heavy cream to a saucepan and heat over medium-high heat until simmering, being careful not to scald or boil.

While the milk mixture is heating, chop the dark chocolate. (For best flavor, use a good quality chocolate that's at least 60 - 70% cacao.)

Once simmering and heated thoroughly, remove from the heat and add the chopped chocolate to the saucepan.

Whisk until smooth.

Pour into small mugs and serve immediately with whipped cream and a little extra chopped chocolate on top.

Chocolate Hot Buttered Rum

Prep: 5 minutes

Total: 5 minutes

INGREDIENTS

2-3 tablespoons Chocolate Hot Buttered Rum Mix recipe HERE

2 1/2 ounces good quality dark rum I used SelvaRey which is actually a cacao rum. SO GOOD. This isn't sponsored, but it's a fun brand. You can use whatever your favorite dark rum is

3 ounces boiling water

3 large marshmallows for garnish optional

INSTRUCTIONS

Spoon 2-3 tablespoons of the Chocolate Hot Buttered Rum Mix into the bottom of your glass.

Pour the rum over the mix.

Top with 3 ounces boiling water (or top to the top of your glass)

Stir to combine. It may take a minute to melt and stir together, but be patient. Deliciousness is coming!

Top with marshmallows if desired and serve warm.

Enjoy!

Vegan Mexican Hot Chocolate

PREP TIME: 2 MINUTES

COOK TIME: 5 MINUTES

TOTAL TIME: 7 MINUTES

SERVES: 2

INGREDIENTS

1 3/4 cups unsweetened vanilla almond milk

½ cup light coconut milk (from the can)

1.5 oz dairy free dark chocolate bar, broken into pieces

1-2 tablespoons unsweetened cocoa powder, depending on your preference

1 teaspoon McCormick ground cinnamon

¼ teaspoon McCormick ground red cayenne pepper

Pinch of salt

1 tablespoon coconut sugar

INSTRUCTIONS

In a small pot, add coconut milk, almond milk, chocolate bar pieces, cocoa powder, cinnamon, cayenne pepper, salt and coconut sugar. Whisk together and bring ingredients to a simmer, then reduce heat to low and simmer for 3-5 minutes to reduce the mixture a bit; stirring occasionally.

Pour into 2 small mugs, then sprinkle with a little ground cinnamon on top, or add a cinnamon stick. Enjoy!

Malted Milk Hot Chocolate

Prep: 10 minutes

Total: 10 minutes

INGREDIENTS

2 cups confectioner's powdered sugar

1 cup unsweetened cocoa

1 cup nonfat dry milk powder

1 1/2 cups malted milk powder chocolate **See note.

2 teaspoons cornstarch

1 teaspoon salt

Milk or hot water to serve

INSTRUCTIONS

Sift all ingredients (except the salt) in a large bowl. Add the salt and whisk all ingredients until thoroughly combined. Transfer to an airtight container and store at room temperature up to 6 months.

To serve, bring 1-cup hot water or milk just to a simmer. Pour hot liquid into a mug and mix in ¼ cup Hot Chocolate Mix (or to taste).

Optional:

Mini marshmallows

Pinch of cayenne pepper or cinnamon

Flavorings (added at time of serving) – vanilla, mint extract, orange extract, raspberry extract

Liqueurs – Irish Cream, Frangelico, Kahlua, Amaretto or your favorite

*Note: For best results, shake the hot chocolate mix to incorporate separated ingredients before each use.

**Note: If regular hot chocolate mix is desired, leave out the malted milk powder and use 2 cups nonfat dry milk powder instead.

Vanilla Mocha Hot Cocoa

prep time: 10 minutes

cook time: 5 minutes

total time: 15 minutes

servings: 4

INGREDIENTS

4 1/2 cups whole milk (or nut milk)

1/3 cup real maple syrup

1/4 cup unsweetened cocoa powder

6 ounces semi-sweet or dark chocolate, chopped (I like to use 72% dark)

1 tablespoon vanilla extract

1 tablespoon instant coffee powder

1 pinch flaky salt

whipped cream, for serving

grated nutmeg or cinnamon (optional)

INSTRUCTIONS

Add the milk, maple syrup, cocoa powder, chocolate, vanilla, coffee powder, and pinch of salt to a large pot. Place the pot over medium low heat until the milk is scalding, but not boiling. Be sure to stir the pot often to make sure nothing is sticking to the bottom and burning.

Once the hot cocoa is steaming, ladle into mugs and dollop with whipped cream. Drink and enjoy!

SLOW COOKER INSTRUCTIONS

Add the milk, maple syrup, cocoa powder, chocolate, vanilla, coffee powder, and pinch of salt to the bowl of your crockpot. Cover and cook on low for 2 hours, stirring occasionally. Switch to warm until ready to serve, up to 2 more hours.

Ladle into mugs and dollop with whipped cream. Drink and enjoy!

Peanut Butter Hot Chocolate

Yield: 2 servings

Prep Time: 5 minutes

Cook Time: 5 minutes

Total Time: 10 minutes

INGREDIENTS:

For hot chocolate:

1-1/2 cups whole milk

1/2 cups semisweet chocolate morsels

1/4 cup creamy peanut butter

For topping:

1 cup cold heavy whipping cream

1 teaspoon Truvia sweetener OR 2 teaspoons sugar

Chocolate Syrup

2 tablespoons melted peanut butter

INSTRUCTIONS

For hot chocolate:

Add milk, chocolate morsels and peanut butter into your high speed blender. I used my Vitamix.

Top the Vitamix and process on high for 4-5 minutes until the mixture is hot and frothy.

Pour hot chocolate into 2 mugs.

For topping:

While your hot chocolate is processing make whipped cream.

In the bowl of an electric mixer add whipping cream and sweetener. Whip until the mixture has reached soft peaks.

Top hot chocolate with equal amount of whipped cream and drizzle on chocolate syrup and melted peanut butter.

Notes: If you do not own a high powered blender just add all hot chocolate ingredients to a small saucepan and warm on the stove over medium heat until hot and creamy.

Peppermint White Hot Chocolate Recipe

Prep Time: 5 MINUTES

Cook Time: 5 MINUTES

Total Time: 10 MINUTES

Servings: 8

INGREDIENTS

3 cups milk

3 cups half & half or light cream

1 1/2 cups white chocolate chips

1 teaspoon vanilla extract

1 teaspoon peppermint extract

crushed candy canes (optional)

INSTRUCTIONS

Combine milk and cream (or half & half) in a large sauce pan over medium heat. Heat, stirring occasionally, until hot throughout. Reduce heat to medium-low.

Add white chocolate and stir until completely melted and incorporated. Stir in vanilla and peppermint extract. Serve with a candy cane on the side of the glass or crushed candy canes around the rim.

Slow Cooker Hot Chocolate

Prep Time: 5 minutes

Cook Time: 2 hours

Total Time: 2 hours 5 minutes

INGREDIENTS

1/4 cup cocoa powder sifted

1 14 ounce can sweetened condensed milk

7 cups milk use whole milk for the creamiest hot chocolate!

1 cup heavy cream can use half and half, but cream gives the best results

1 teaspoon vanilla extract

1 cup semisweet chocolate chips

1 cup milk chocolate chips

Marshmallows, whipped cream, chocolate chips etc. for garnish

INSTRUCTIONS

Place the cocoa powder, condensed milk, heavy cream, milk, vanilla extract, semisweet chocolate chips and milk chocolate chips in a slow cooker. Stir to combine.

Cook on LOW for 2 hours. Stir well until thoroughly mixed. Turn the slow cooker to the KEEP WARM setting until you're ready to serve the hot chocolate. Garnish with marshmallows and/or whipped cream if desired.

Nutella Hot Chocolate

cook time: 5 MINUTES

total time: 5 MINUTES

yield: 1 CUP

INGREDIENTS

2 Tbsp. Nutella

1 cup milk (any kind)

optional toppings: whipped cream, marshmallows, chocolate syrup, chocolate shavings

INSTRUCTIONS

Heat milk in a small saucepan over medium-high heat until steaming (not boiling), stirring occasionally.

Add in the Nutella, and whisk until dissolved.

Serve immediately, either plain or with your desired toppings.

White Hot Chocolate

YIELDS:10 servings

TOTAL TIME:0 hours 30 mins

INGREDIENTS

4 c. whole milk

12 oz. white chocolate, finely chopped

1 tsp. vanilla bean paste (or 1/2 tsp. pure vanilla extract)

1/8 tsp. kosher salt

Pink gel food coloring

1 recipe 7-Minute Frosting

INSTRUCTIONS

Combine milk, chocolate, vanilla, and salt in a medium saucepan. Cook over medium heat, whisking constantly, until mixture is hot and chocolate is melted and smooth (do not let boil), 6 to 8 minutes.

Add a few drops of food coloring to frosting and stir twice to create a swirl pattern; carefully transfer to a piping bag. Pipe on top of hot chocolate in mugs.

Sugar Cookie Hot Chocolate

prep time: 10 minutes

cook time: 10 minutes

total time: 20 minutes

servings: 4 mugs

INGREDIENTS

4 1/2 cups whole milk

2/3 cup sweetened condensed milk

1/4 cup cocoa powder

6 ounces semi-sweet or dark chocolate chopped

1 tablespoon vanilla extract

1/4 teaspoon almond extract

whipped cream marshmallows, sugar cookies and or coarse sugar, for topping

INSTRUCTIONS

Add the milk, sweetened condensed milk, cocoa powder, chocolate, vanilla, and almond extract (if using) to a large pot. Place the pot over medium low heat until the milk is scalding, but not boiling. Be sure to stir the pot often to make sure nothing is sticking to the bottom and burning.Once the hot chocolate is steaming, ladle into mugs and dollop with whipped cream. Add marshmallows, cookies and a sprinkle of sugar if desired. Drink!

Slow Cooker Pumpkin Spice Hot Chocolate

Prep: 5 minutes

Cook: 2 hours

Total: 2 hours 5 minutes

INGREDIENTS

2 cups heavy cream

4 cups milk

1 14oz can sweetened condensed milk

1 cup pumpkin puree

1 tablespoon pumpkin pie spice

1 1/2 cups Stoli Gluten Free Vodka you can use more or less to taste

2 cups or about 10 ounces good quality semi sweet chocolate chips

marshmallows or whipped cream for garnish optional

INSTRUCTIONS

Add the cream, milk, sweetened condensed milk, pumpkin puree, pumpkin pie spice, and vodka to a slow cooker. Use a whisk to combine as fully as possible. Pour in the chocolate chips.

Set the slow cooker on low for 2 hours or until chocolate is fully melted and mixture is hot to your liking.

Top with marshmallows or whipped cream and serve!

Enjoy!

Blackberry Hot Chocolate

Cook Time: 10 minutes

Total Time: 10 minutes

Servings: 4 servings

INGREDIENTS

200 g/ 7oz blackberries (fresh or frozen)

3 tbsp icing (confectionary) sugar

1 tbsp water (if using fresh blackberries)

1/2 tsp vanilla extract

720 ml/ 3 cups whole milk (or non-dairy equivalent)

120 g/ 4 1/4oz dark chocolate

Optional Garnish (recommended)

Whipped cream

Mini marshmallows

Extra blackberries

INSTRUCTIONS

If using frozen blackberries allow to defrost in a small saucepan for 30 minutes. Once softened add the icing sugar and cook, on a moderate heat, for around 5 minutes until the blackberries are soft and squishy

If using fresh blackberries, cook as above with the icing sugar and a tablespoon of water

Push the cooked blackberries and juices through a sieve to create a coulis. Scrape the thick pulp from the outside of the sieve into the coulis as you go. Discard the seeds

Heat the milk until scalding

Meanwhile chop the chocolate and drop into the base of a blender, along with the vanilla extract

Pour the hot milk over the chocolate. Allow to sit for 1 minute

Reserve 1 tbsp of the blackberry coulis and put the rest into the blender

Blitz until the chocolate has melted and the drink is frothy

Sweeten to taste and reheat if necessary

Pour into mugs and top with whipped cream, marshmallows, a drizzle of the reserved blackberry coulis and a blackberry

Serve immediately

Notes

Leftover hot chocolate can be cooled, stored in the fridge and reheated within 2 days. Stir well to re-blend the ingredients

Snickerdoodle Hot Cocoa

INGREDIENTS

3 c. half & half *can substitute with fat free half & half or lowfat milk

⅔ c. white chocolate chopped

1 cinnamon stick

½ tsp. vanilla

½ tsp. cinnamon

⅛ tsp. Nutmeg

INSTRUCTIONS

Combine ¼ c. half & half, white chocolate, and cinnamon stick in a small saucepan.

Heat on low, stirring constantly, until white chocolate is melted.

Add remaining half & half and spices and heat through.

Remove cinnamon stick before serving.

Cookies and Cream Hot Chocolate

Yield: 2

INGREDIENTS:

2 cups whole milk

1/2 cup hot chocolate mix (homemade or store-bought)

6 Oreo cookies

whipped cream for garnish, optional

additional crushed oreos for garnish, optional

INSTRUCTIONS:

In a small saucepan, heat milk until very hot but not boiling. Alternately, you can heat the milk in the microwave. In the pitcher of your blender, add hot milk, oreos and hot chocolate mix. Pulse until cookies are completely ground and there are no large pieces. Pour into two mugs and garnish with whipped cream and crushed cookies, if desired.

Cookies and Cream Hot Chocolate is best served immediately.

Red Velvet Hot Cocoa

Prep: 5 mins

Cooking time: 10 mins

Total: 15 mins

Servings: 1

INGREDIENTS

For The Hot Cocoa:

1 glass (250ml) milk (optional: plant-based)

60-70g dark chocolate

1 tsp maple syrup

1 ½ tsp red food coloring

For the white cream on top:

4 tbsp whipped cream

1 tbsp powdered sugar

½ tsp almond extract

INSTRUCTIONS

In a saucepan boil water over high heat. Turn to medium and place a metal bowl on top of it.

Crush the chocolate into small pieces and add them to the metal bowl. Stir while they melt.

Slowly pour the milk into the melted chocolate. Stir well.

Mix in the red food coloring and maple syrup. Stir for one-two more minutes, then remove from heat. Transfer the hot cocoa to a mug.

Whip the cream together with the powdered sugar. Add the almond extract while whipping.

Add and shape the whipped cream over the hot chocolate.

Cheesecake Hot Chocolate

yield: 2

prep time: 5 MINUTES

cook time: 10 MINUTES

total time: 15 MINUTES

INGREDIENTS

1 cup milk

1/4 teaspoon vanilla extract

2 ounces white chocolate, chopped

2 ounces cream cheese, room temperature* and cut into 16 pieces

Graham cracker crumbs and whipped cream, for garnish

INSTRUCTIONS

In a medium saucepan, warm up the milk over medium heat until hot but not boiling. Turn the heat down to low then whisk in the vanilla cream cheese until melted. Whisk in the white chocolate until melted and smooth. Serve immediately** with whipped cream and graham cracker crumbs on top, if desired.

NOTES

The cream cheese needs to be at room temperature or even slightly softer (without risking food safety). Otherwise, the hot chocolate mixture may become lumpy. If it does become lumpy, you can use the blender to help smooth it.

*The drink does thicken as it cools down. Just heat it back up in the microwave.

Frozen Hot Chocolate

Prep: 5 minutes

Cook: 5 minutes

Total: 10 minutes

INGREDIENTS

1/2 cups chocolate chips or 4 oz of chocolate

2 tsp. hot cocoa mix

1 1/2 Tbsp sugar

1 1/2 cup milk divided

3 cup ice cubes

sweetened whipped cream

chocolate sprinkles optional

INSTRUCTIONS

Chop chocolate into small pieces and melt in a glass container in microwave for 10-20 second intervals until melted.

Add in hot cocoa mix and sugar to melted chocolate. Mix until blended.

Add in 1/2 C milk, stir until smooth. Allow to cool to room temperature

In blender, place remaining milk, cooled chocolate mixture and ice cubes

Blend on high speed until smooth and consistency of a frozen daiquiri

Pour into mugs and top with whipped cream and sprinkles.

Peppermint White Chocolate

prep time: 2 MINUTES

cook time: 8 MINUTES

total time: 10 MINUTES

yield: 4 SERVINGS

INGREDIENTS

4 cups of milk of your choice

8 oz. white chocolate, chopped into small pieces (or white chocolate chips)

1 teaspoon vanilla extract

1/2 teaspoon peppermint extract (or more/less to taste)

optional toppings: whipped cream, crushed peppermints, marshmallows

INSTRUCTIONS

Stir the milk and chopped white chocolate together in a medium saucepan. Cook over medium-low heat, stirring occasionally, until the mixture comes to a simmer and the chocolate is melted. (Do not let it come to a boil or let the chocolate burn on the bottom.) Remove from heat and stir in vanilla and peppermint extract.

Serve warm, with optional toppings if desired.

White Hot Chocolate

cook time: 15 MINUTES

total time: 15 MINUTES

yield: 5 CUPS

INGREDIENTS

4 cups of milk of your choice (or you can substitute heavy cream or half and half, or do a mixture)

1 tsp. vanilla extract, store-bought or homemade

8 oz. white chocolate, chopped into small pieces (or white chocolate chips)

whipped cream or marshmallows for topping

INSTRUCTIONS

Stir together milk, vanilla and chopped white chocolate in a medium saucepan. Cook over medium-low heat, stirring occasionally, until the white hot chocolate comes to a simmer. (Do not let it come to a boil.) Remove from heat and serve immediately, topped with whipped cream or marshmallows if desired.

Hot Chocolate Float

Yield: 2 servings

INGREDIENTS

8 ounces prepared hot chocolate

1/2 cup of your favorite ice cream

Whipped cream for garnish

57

INSTRUCTIONS

Use your favorite hot chocolate mix to make a glass (about 8 ounces) of hot chocolate. I use the k-cups for my Keurig but you can also use 8 ounces of water with your favorite hot chocolate packet or 8 ounces of milk and some homemade hot chocolate mix.

Pour an equal amount of the hot chocolate in two mugs. (The pictures shown are one very large mug, but it serves 2.)

Place ¼ cup (1 scoop) of ice cream in each mug. Top with whipped cream and/or sprinkles and/or chocolate sauce.

Serve immediately.

Slow Cooker Salted Caramel Hot Chocolate

Prep Time: 5 MINUTES

Cook Time: 2 HOURS

Total Time: 2 HOURS 5 MINUTES

Servings: 8

INGREDIENTS

2 cups semi sweet OR milk chocolate chips (milk chocolate chips will yield a much richer flavor - I like to use a combination of both!)

1/2 cup caramels, unwrapped

4 cups milk

2 cups heavy cream

1 teaspoon vanilla

1/2 teaspoon fine sea salt (for regular non-salted caramel hot chocolate, leave this out)

optional: whipping cream, caramel sauce (like caramel ice cream topping)

INSTRUCTIONS

Add chocolate chips, caramels, milk, heavy cream, and vanilla to the slow cooker. Cover and cook on low for 2 hours.

Stir the hot chocolate. If the chocolate chips or caramels are not completely melted, cover and allow to cook for 20-30 minutes longer. When ready to serve, stir in the sea salt. Serve hot with whipped cream and additional caramel sauce if desired.

S'mores Hot Chocolate

REP TIME: 5 minutes

COOK TIME: 5 minutes

TOTAL TIME: 10 minutes

INGREDIENTS

2 cups milk (any kind // dairy-free for vegan)

1 cup water (or sub more milk)

¼ cup cocoa powder

2 Tbsp light chocolate syrup

2 Tbsp sugar

1/4 tsp non-bitter stevia (or add 1-2 Tbsp more sugar to taste)

1 pinch salt

Graham crackers (crushed // for lining rim - gluten-free for GF eaters)

½ cup marshmallows (ensure vegan-friendliness)

INSTRUCTIONS

Preheat oven to low broil and move oven rack to the second from the top (high enough up to broil your marshmallows). Place baking sheet on rack.

Heat milk and water in a saucepan over medium heat until warmed through - about 5 minutes. Be careful not to overheat or scald.

Add cocoa powder, chocolate syrup, sugar, stevia and salt and whisk vigorously until thoroughly combined.

Meanwhile, take a few marshmallows and rub them around the top of your mugs so the graham crackers will stick. Then, dip mug in graham cracker crumbs until well lined. You could also add some graham cracker crumbs to the bottom of your mug for extra graham flavor.

Pour in hot chocolate and top with 1/4 cup marshmallows each. Carefully set mugs on the baking sheet in the oven and broil marshmallows until browned, watching carefully as to not let them burn.

Carefully remove from the oven with a towel and serve with holders or a small towel to protect hand from heat (they should cool quickly for handling). Top with a drizzle of chocolate syrup and extra graham cracker crumbs for serving (optional).

Notes

* Adjust flavors before serving, adding more chocolate or sugar if you prefer.

* Also, you could add a shot of Kahlua or Bailey's to make it a boozy hot chocolate.

Spicy Maple Cinnamon Hot Chocolate

Prep Time: 5 mins

Cook Time: 10 mins

Total Time: 15 mins

INGREDIENTS

2 1/2 cups whole milk

6 tablespoons Dutch process cocoa

2 tablespoons maple syrup (add up to 2 more tablespoons to taste)

1/2 teaspoon ground cinnamon

1/2 teaspoon chili powder

1/4 teaspoon ground cayenne

pinch sea salt

1/2 cup heavy whipping cream (optional)

cinnamon sticks for garnish (optional)

INSTRUCTIONS

Pour milk into a medium-sized sauce pan and set over medium-low heat. Whisk in chocolate, maple syrup, and spices. Continue whisking occasionally until milk is hot and steamy. Taste, and add more maple syrup if needed.

Meanwhile, whisk heavy whipping cream to soft peaks.

Pour steaming hot chocolate into mugs, add a dollop of whipped cream and a cinnamon stick, and finish with a pinch of chili powder.

Note: This recipe makes for a very chocolaty drink, dilute with more milk if it's too much. It's also pretty easy on the sweet stuff, so add a few more glugs of maple syrup for a sweeter sip.

Printed in Great Britain
by Amazon